Merry xmas
Charlie

This book is de
Christine an
Love you l

ISBN: 0-9552053-0-1

Cover design and layout by Direct Print Ltd. Tel: (01) 8740433

This book is typeset in Palatino 12pt.

Printed by Direct Print Ltd.

1st Published December 2005 by Gary Grange

Introduction

Hi! My name is Gary Grange I'm a 43 year old separated man with two wonderful children Christine aged 15 and Adam aged 7. I'm also fortunate that my ex-wife Elizabeth hasn't turned into a bunny boiler, (I'll endeavour to explain that later) and we still remain friends.

My qualifications writing this book are a masters in creating messy situations, and a PHD in the skills required to survive them.

Over the course of this book I'll be taking a light-hearted, sometimes cynical look at the behaviour of men and women, and the myths they've cultivated about themselves to help them disguise their true natures. Some of the views expressed in this book may seem a little strange at first, as political correctness was not my main concern.

Enjoy!

CONTENTS

To help you gain some insight into the content of this book. I've compiled a list of twenty questions which deal directly with the subject matter of this book. If you find any of these questions and answers either, unpleasant or painful, I'd highly recommend that you stop reading this book immediately and head on back to oblivion!

1) Are you a male chauvinist? Yes/No or only when you're out with the boys!
Answer..........
2) How would you described yourself? As rich, good-looking or funny?
Answer...........
3) When did you first get married? In your twenties, thirties or you find it too painful to think about!
Answer.............
4) When was your last argument? Last week, last month or is it continuous!
Answer.............
5) What do you argue mostly about? Money, directions or sex!
Answer.............
6) How would you rate your sex life? Good, bad or your memory doesn't stretch that far back!
Answer............
7) Would you wife swap? Yes/ No or only on a permanent bases!
Answer.............

8) Were you ever unfaithful? Yes/ No or you've never been caught!

Answer............

9) Does your partner have a big bum? Yes/No or it depends who's asking!

Answer............

10) Is your partner a good driver? Yes/No or only on straight roads!

Answer............

11) Does you partner play golf? Yes/No or she plays the downhill par threes quite well!

Answer...........

12) Does your partner talk too much? Yes/No or only between air intakes!

Answer...........

13) Did you have sex on your first date? Yes/No or was the conversation too rivetting to be interrupted!

Answer...........

14) Does your partner seem happy? Yes/No or never!

Answer..........

15) Have you slept with your partner's best friend? Yes/No or are you still trying!

Answer.........

16) Do you fantasize about other women? Yes/No or it's confined to your partner's best friend!

Answer...........

17) Has your partner changed over the years? Yes/No or only in size!

Answer.....

18) Is your life boring? Yes/No or only the odd occasion you're partner has nothing for you to do!
Answer......

19) How does your present partner compare to previous ones? Good/Bad or much the same but a lot younger!
Answer...........

If you found any of these questions too difficult to answer and you want more information before completing your answers. Then read on!

"MAMMY'S BOY"

The first introduction a man gets to women is through his mother. This is a woman who minds and guides him, cooks and cleans for him, and more often than not, places a magic drawer in his bedroom that allows him to drop all his dirty clothes on his bedroom floor and have them miraculously reappearing eight hours later, washed, pressed and neatly folded back in the magic drawer.

Now if this was the type of care and attention men received from every woman they considered "special" that would be fine, but unfortunately nothing could be further from the truth.

So let's see what really happens when mammy's boy decides to take daddy's girl on a one way journey through the tunnel of love.

Its time for the truth!

Let's hope you can handle it?

"If only they were all like your mammy"

"THE IDEAL MAN"

We'll begin our story by first analysing exactly what it is that women want from men and their chances of ever finding the perfect match.

Did you ever wonder what constitutes the ideal man? If you've ever taken your ear plugs out for long enough to listen to what women have to say on the subject, it shouldn't be too difficult for you to figure it out.

The most important quality by all accounts is mans ability to make a woman laugh i.e. Billy Connolly or Mike Myers. In second place are good looks i.e. a Brad Pitt or Colin Farrell look-alike will do fine! Thirdly he must have a good income 100/200K per year i.e. a banker! Fourth he must be very good in bed "but only when he's required" i.e. a porn star! Fifth he must be able to empathise with her when she has problems, while never attempting to solve any of them i.e. psychologist! And last but by no means least a good home maker i.e. Mrs Doubtfire!

Now after reading the above is there anything about yourself that could be immediately changed to help the women of your dreams become a bit happier? Or have you just realised that the reason for women's unhappiness is quite simple, there's just not enough good looking, rich male psychologists to go round them all.

Let's finish with this thought!

Can you imagine if a man waited until he found a

woman, who was good looking i.e. Pamela Anderson or Paris Hilton! Funny i.e. Pamela Anderson or Paris Hilton telling jokes, domesticated i.e. Pamela Anderson or Paris Hilton cooking, preferably nude! wealthy i.e. Pamela Anderson or Paris Hilton anywhere nude! before he'd even consider the thought of getting married!

*It could be the "ideal" solution
to all his domestic problems.*

"Ideal for whom"

The five secrets of the perfect relationship:

1) It is important to have a woman who can cook and clean.

*2) It is important to have a woman
who can make you laugh.*

3) It is important to have a woman you can trust.

4) It is important to have a woman who is good in bed.

*5) And it is very very important that none
of these women ever meet.*

"FORTUNE TELLERS, TAROT CARDS AND HOROSCOPES"

Why do so many women constantly worry about their future? The main focus of which seems to be centered around tall dark handsome strangers and money.

It seems the only way women will ever find true happiness, is when they know absolutely everything, which includes, what's going to happen in the future.

The main questions women ask fortune tellers are as follows: "when will prince charming be arriving on his horse?", "when will we be moving house?", "will it take me long to get over him?", "am I due a lottery win?"

Unbeknown to many women who visit fortune tellers is the little known fact that fortune tellers are capable of influencing all their future decisions. Take Mary for example! Mary goes to a fortune teller to try and learn if the love of her life is on his way. The fortune teller looks at some cards and tells Mary a "small blonde guy" is going to enter her life very soon, and she'll eventually marry him. Believe it or not! As soon as Mary leaves the fortune teller she's on the lookout for "Tiny Tim".

When she's on a night out with the girls, she'll purposely ignore every tall guy that approaches her and will instead concentrate all her efforts on finding the "the blonde midget".

When she eventually finds a guy who matches the fortune teller's description, immediately she'll go into a state of panic and start wondering could this possibly be him?

Suddenly! Mary decides to take a whole new approach to men and she sets about trying to attract "Tiny Tim's" attention.

Because Mary is not used to doing any approach work herself, she relies heavily on the hit and miss methods used by generations of women to attract men i.e. staring and telepathy.

But Mary is fortunate tonight as although "Tiny Tim" is short sighted, he compensates for his by being a terrific mind reader! He suddenly plucks up the courage to approach Mary, but he's very nervous as he normally gets the "fuck off squirt" routine before he gets any chance to tell his best one liner's. But tonight it's different and instead he finds a woman who's only too happy to laugh at his stupid jokes "well at least smile anyway", and amazingly she actually seems interested in what he has to say. After he's had Mary laughing for a while he decides to take a chance on asking her out. To his utter amazement, Mary agrees immediately, unfortunately the poor guy doesn't realise it at the time, but Mary is now convinced she's met her future husband just as fortune teller had predicted on her recent visit.

The next day she tells her friends about the great guy she met the previous night and the fortune teller's prediction. Next thing you know her friends go to the same fortune teller for some guidance on their futures. A year or so later all the girls accidentally bump in to each other on a night out with their boyfriends. I say accidentally, because none of the girls had been in contact with each other since Mary met her future husband. To the utter amazement of the girls they suddenly realised all their boyfriends looked exactly the same i.e. They're all small with blonde hair!

As Mary and her friends study the three blonde midgets sitting in the corner with their legs dangling over the seats, they're suddenly struck with the thought of tall dark handsome strangers. Immediately they unanimously agree to give the fortune teller one last chance.

This proves three things

1) Women really don't like small guys.

2) Nothing they say one day has any bearing on what they might think the next.

3) They reserve the right to deny anything they've said after 24 hours.

"Delusions"

"LIBERATION"

You may find this hard to believe! But it wasn't always as easy as it is today to find somebody willing to indulge in a bit of "how's your father", some "slapping and tickling". Believe it or not, previous generations of men had to marry a woman before they had any chance of cancelling their weekly appointment with palm and her five sisters.

But today, thanks to women's lib and the modern females ability to consume large quantities of alcohol, this problem has virtually disappeared. In fact men are so confident these days of finding a willing woman on a night out, they don't even bother to approach one until it's practically closing time. Now we're not talking super models here. More the plain looking, overweight, slightly pissed type, whose only real chance of ever being able to claim "victim status", is if she finds a man brave enough to administer some "coyote treatment" to himself i.e. "a coyote will bite off its own leg to free itself from a trap" if he's unfortunate enough to fall asleep post-shag with his arm pinned under her head.

Now this type of behaviour does have its draw backs, as it has turned what was once considered dining at a fancy restaurant, into something more appropriately described as a late night "snack box" from the local "fast food" restaurant. Now you might think my description of things is a little unfair? So let's take a look at what generally happens in the lead up to what's commonly know as a one night stand/shag.

A woman meets a guy in a pub/club, a guy she's probably never set eyes on before, a guy she takes home to continue the deep meaningful conversation they began twenty minutes earlier. A guy who disappears by sunrise leaving her slightly panicked and suffering symptoms of "drug induced" memory loss. This causes her to wonder if she did or if she didn't? She then heads to her local doctor for the morning after pill, just in case she did.

Before she ends up being right once again!

All men are the same?

"The fast food experience"

"CONTRACEPTION"

The following is a list of some of the favourite contraception methods used by men and their effectiveness.

Method (1) - The Marshmallow

This method relies heavily on the man drinking 10-12 pints of beer. It's effective for two reasons **1st** the man is unable to converse properly with the object of his desire **2nd** if by some miracle he can still talk and can convince her, that he's not actually drunk, but has indeed just arrived from another planet. His inability to wake the little head, before the big head falls asleep, gives this method a 90% success rate.

Method (2) - Withdrawal

This method is strictly for those men who like to gamble as it's based totally on timing. The effectiveness of this method is very limited, due to men's inability to arrive anywhere on time. 50% success rate

Method (3) - Condoms

This method relies heavily on luck - **1st** the man has to find a condom machine that works **2nd** he must have the correct change available **3rd** he must be careful they don't burst, slip off, or that he "accidently" removes them for resuscitation purposes. The correct application gives 95% protection but in reality it's more 70%

Method (4) - The Snip

This method is the most effective known to man. The man turns up at the doctor's surgery and produces his tackle. The doctor makes two small incisions in the bag containing his jewels. He then removes two small tubes, which he then cuts and solders before replacing them back in the bag. A couple of stitches either side completes the procedure. This method is 100% effective but has its draw backs i.e. it's difficult to find a doctor at 3am who's willing to carry out this procedure and by the way its painful.

Method (5) - Rely on your partner

This is the most common approach taken by men, as it allows them freedom to concentrate on the job at hand, without having any responsibility for the outcome of their actions, well, not for at least nine months anyway. Long-term effectiveness 20%

"There's no such thing as a free ride"

"MEETING MISS RIGHT"

There are many different places for men to introduce themselves to the members of opposite sex with some of the most frequently used locations being the local pub or nightclub.

It's a well known fact that most men on a night out need to consume large amounts of alcohol before they would consider approaching any member of the opposite sex. There are three main reasons for this: First the man needs to build up some much needed "dutch courage". Second, he needs alcohol to help insulate his feelings against the many refusals that will surly come his way. And third he needs to give himself lots of time to survey his surroundings before deciding which potential victim to make his move on. Sorry did I say victim! What I actually mean is potential long term partner.

When he's finished surveying all the potential long term partners and he eventually spots what seems in his eyes anyway, a nice friendly looking girl, he decides to make his move to try and confirm what his eyes have been telling him.

But more often than not he only ends up confirming what his optician has been telling him for years i.e. he defiantly needs glasses. Unfortunately for him,the nice charming girl that he'd hoped for, turns out to be a half pissed miss cynical, who's spent the entire evening sitting on her large "alcohol inflated" arse waiting for some tall, handsome guy to arrive and sweep her off her feet and guess what? He's defiantly not him.

Now not all women fit this description and some have very good reason to be wary of strange men who enter their company uninvited, asking the same old questions and who, unfortunately "for any nice guys out there", don't seem to know how to take a hint and therefore piss everybody off, by overstaying their imaginary welcome.

To help those men out there who don't want to be branded as a complete tosser by members of the opposite sex, I've enlisted the help of some well known moochers to explain some of the various tactics they employ while they're out for a night on the pull.

First and foremost is not being too fussy "as too fussy means no pussy! 2nd is to try and smell nice 3rd is develop a hard neck 4th is don't take refusals personally 5th try not to brag 6th learn to empathise 7th give some compliments 8th tell a few jokes 9th lie

When you add this to any alcohol your target, (Sorry I mean "potential long term partner",) may have already consumed, "bingo" you're almost certain to score.

But if you fail on your first attempt don't worry, as this is where a hard neck and your ability not to take refusals personally come into play. Now instead of feeling rejected, you just carry on moving from table to table, using the exact same script, approaching every miss cynical along the way, until eventually you find one who's either too drunk or too desperate to care.

So lads if you want to prevent yourself from being branded a "tosser" by the opposite sex, all you need to do is find yourself a corner to stand in and say absolutely nothing.

Now if any women happen to read this and they want some advice on how they prevent themselves becoming a victim of one of these stereo typical men, here are a few tips

1) Try concentrating your efforts on the men who spend their nights standing in corners.

2) Don't rely on men having good eyesight or being telepathic when trying to attract their attention.

3) Instead of sitting waiting for Mr Right to arrive and sweep you off your feet, why not try and do some of the approach work yourselves. As the way things are going in the arse department girls, a white elephant might be a more appropriate steed for Mr Right to ride in on.

"It's a numbers game?"

"FALLING IN LOVE"

If you've never had anything but good experiences from falling in love please turn immediately to the next chapter. But if your one of those less fortunate people that always seem to get hurt when they fall in love, Please continue.

Have you ever stopped to wonder why the word "fall" is used in front of the word love, and not something more positive like the word "lifted".

Think of it this way! When the word fall is normally placed in front of a word is usually placed there as a word of warning i.e. Careful you don't fall down, careful you don't fall off, or careful not to fall out. Now with this in mind why are so many people surprised when they get hurt after falling head over heels in love with somebody they hardly know.

Imagine for a moment if everybody considered falling in love with another person as serious as finding a partner to help them climb a mountain.

Do you think everybody would head straight to the local pub or nightclub to find a suitable climbing partner, and judge their endurance and mobility skills by their ability to drink large quantities of alcohol while still being able to walk and talk?

Or would you **(1st)** make a list of the skills are required to climb a mountain **(2nd)** when you find a suitable climbing partner, don't trust anything to chance, get their climbing skills verified! **(3rd)** climb a few small mountains at first as this will help you to develop the trust you will need for the more difficult climbs ahead **(4th)** make sure you're capable of climbing alone, in case your new climbing partner decides to quit, during a difficult part of the climb, leaving you to continue climbing on your own **(5th)** accept the possibility that you could be hurt during a climb, and be prepared to take your share of the responsibility for any failure to complete it.

So before deciding to go climbing anywhere, it might be a good idea if you make a list of exactly what is it you want from a climbing partner, as it just might prevent you from being badly hurt in some unforeseen fall.

"Respect"

"MR COMMITMENT"

Every woman knows? Or at least they should do! That a mere mention of the word "commitment" is enough to send most single men scampering towards the nearest emergency exit.

This irrational fear of commitment, which seems to plague the single man, is all the more difficult to understand when you consider the immense benefits of commitment to any relationship.

How can anybody in their right mind think, Coming and going as they please, making all their own decisions, meeting loads of different women and spending all their money on themselves, could possibly compensate them for the immense benefits they'll receive from making a commitment.

Think about it! Never being alone again, always having somebody concerned about your whereabouts, all your decisions being made for you, plus the added benefit of somebody organising all your finances and helping you decide the best way to spend your money.

Now before you get too excited about the prospect of making a commitment, it wouldn't be fair if I didn't mention some of the risks involved in doing so.

With this in mind let's take a quick look at some problems you might encounter in the unlikely event of you deciding to renege on your part of the commitment.

For a start if you commit yourself to somebody and

decide later that it wasn't such a good idea, you might be required to forfeit your living accommodation, but as there's loads of rental property available this shouldn't cause too many problems. Then there's the little matter of regular access to your children, but you've probably no intention of having any, so that's another problem solved. Now the only thing left to worry about is where to put your possessions, but as your new accommodation will come fully furnished and long term storage is both expensive and inconvenient, your lack of possessions could be a blessing in disguise!

So why don't you just do it!!!

*"Commitment isn't a problem
but its failure certainly is"*

Why does divorced barbie cost twice as much as single barbie?
Because she comes with Kens house and car

"WRITTEN IN THE STARS"

There's a great deal of scepticism surrounding birth signs and the affects they have on our everyday life.

Without delving too deeply into the subject I've written a short synopsis on the personality traits of each birth sign. It might be a good idea if you study the personality traits of your partners birth sign, as this information can be useful during an argument.

It might also prevent a future trip to the divorce courts by allowing you to decide in advance, the type of personality traits you'd like to find in any long term partner or more importantly the ones you wouldn't.

The information I've supplied on birth signs is short and sweet unlike the relationship you'll have with a person whose personality traits are no match for yours i.e. long and arduous.

"It just might be written in the stars"

AQUARIUS - JANUARY 21 - FEBRUARY 19

Positive traits = Tolerance, independence, perception
Negative traits = Detachment, individualistic, carefree

Personality = They are independent and don't take kindly to being told what to do. They are easy going but hard workers. They analyze situations extremely well but can be considered aloof. Their behaviour can seem somewhat strange to the outside world

Famous Aquarians = Oprah Winfrey, Abraham Lincoln, Bob Marley

Summary = They treasure their own space.

PISCES - FEBRUARY 20 - MARCH 20

Positive traits = Creative, motivated, perceptive
Negative traits = Arrogance, self pity, rage

Personality = They are quite sensitive, this sensitivity can easily turn to feelings of self pity. They are intuitive and proud but they're also susceptible to substance abuse.

Famous Pisceans = Lisa Minnelli, Elizabeth Taylor, Michelangelo

Summary = Emotionally challenging but certainly not short on excitement.

ARIES - MARCH 21 - APRIL 20

Positive traits = Enterprising, talented, spontaneous
Negative traits = Domineering, self righteous, blunt

Personality = They're perpetual motion and impulsive. They have a habit of saying the wrong thing at the wrong time. There's a child like naivety about them but be assured they are no pushovers. They are talented and like being in the driving seat, even if it's not their car.

Famous Aries = General Patton, Leonardo de Vinci, Hans Christian Andersen

Summary = This one will tire you out, just watching them move.

TAURUS - APRIL 21 - MAY 21

Positive traits = Patience, industrious, sensual
Negative traits = Stubbornness, selfishness, inflexible

Personality = They calculate their way through life, they have a tendency to stray, they are very secretive and can seem slightly paranoid to outside observers. They have excellent observation skills and prize their possessions.

Famous Taureans = Jack Nicholson, Saddam Hussein, Elizabeth 2

Summary = The strong silent type who insist on having it their way.

GEMINI - MAY 22 - JUNE 21

Positive traits = Versatility, quick-witted, stamina.
Negative traits = Self deception, superficial, indecisive.

Personality = They are sharp and quick witted. They possess great stamina which complements their adventurous lifestyles. They need other peoples company but are fickle when it comes to attachment. They bore easily and need constant stimulation. They need a strong partner to guide them

Famous Gemini's = Jacques Cousteau, The Marquis de Sade, Bob Hope

Summary = If you can put up with their constant need for change, their stamina will look after the rest.

CANCER - JUNE 22 - JULY23

Positives traits = Insightful, caring, tenacious
Negatives traits = Moody, hypersensitive, irritable

Personality = They enjoy their creature comforts. They are loyal friends but like to work alone. They dislike constraints and guard their privacy. They are persuasive in arguments but will fight tenaciously when the need arises. They won't show their feelings unless the mood takes them.

Famous Cancers = Julius Caesar, Nelson Mandela, Lady Diana.

Summary = If you can tolerate their mood swings, you certainly won't be disappointed.

LEO - JULY 23 - AUGUST 23

Positive traits = Warm hearted, honourable, courageous
Negative traits = Vanity, inflexibility, arrogance

Personality = They are strong and self assured, they are warm hearted and good friends, they like the nice things in life especially where their home is concerned, appearance is everything and being in charge is essential.

Famous Leos = Madonna, Mick Jagger, Napoleon Bonaparte

Summary = Give them your full attention or else.

VIRGO - AUGUST 24 - SEPTEMBER 22

Positive traits = Practical, logical, awareness
Negative traits = Critical, cleanliness, rigidity

Personality = They are extremely meticulous in all aspects of their life, they're constantly analyzing and thinking about the future, cleanliness and organisation is their middle name. They enjoy a good laugh but are careful how you say things as they are inclined to take things literally.

Famous Virgos = Mother Teresa, Stephan king, Sophia Loren

Summary = If you like organisation, I'm sure you'll enjoy their direct approach.

LIBRA - SEPTEMBER 23 - OCTOBER 22

Positive traits = Charm, stability, good humoured
Negative traits = Procrastinate, indecisive, judgmental

Personality = They like to talk; they are slow to make decisions for themselves, they analyze things from every angle. They adjust their opinions to suite the situation. They have strong views which they don't mind expressing. They like to take things slowly as they can't stand being pressurised.

Famous Librans = Margaret Thatcher, Mahatma Gandhi, Bob Geldof

Summary = You'll need to be a good listener.

SCORPIO - OCTOBER 23 - NOVEMBER 21

Positive traits = Dedicated, industrious, trustworthy
Negative traits = Vengeful, self-centred, suspicious

Personality = They're hard working and trusty individuals who like to be kept busy; they seem confident to the outside world but have a need to control. They are cautious regarding money and are susceptible to bouts of self destruction.

Famous Scorpios = Diego Maradonna, Marie Antoinette, Shah of Iran

Summary = Be careful not to rub this one the wrong way.

SAGITTARIUS - NOVEMBER 23 - DECEMBER 21

Positive traits = Honourable, understanding, caretakers
Negative traits = Idealistic, outspoken, contradiction

Personality = They are very independent; they love to travel and are constantly on the move. They have great self belief and a very positive outlook. They have very idealistic points of view which are not always expressed in the kindest of manner.

Famous Sagittarians = Sinead O'Connor, Howard Hughes, Winston Churchill

Summary = They certainly don't take kindly to being tied down.

CAPRICORN - DECEMBER 22 - JANUARY 20

Positive traits = Ambitious, competitive, entertaining
Negative traits = Pretentious, controlling, insecurity

Personality = They are the consummate salesperson, they are dedicated to achievement, they are generous and entertaining hosts, they have a tendency to be bossy and are not inclined to heed advice. They are very competitive

Famous Capricorns = Mohammed Ali, Martin Luther king, Elvis Presley

Summary = If you'd like patience and persistence, you certainly won't be disappointed.

"LEGAL ADVICE"

The normal procedure for two individuals signing a legally binding contract is for both parties to seek independent legal advice on the terms and conditions of that contract.

The reason for this is quite simple, the solicitors will give their client independent advice on any potential problems regarding the contract. A termination clause will be inserted into the contract to protect both parties against any unforeseen changes in their circumstances.

Also a detailed list of the terms and conditions of the contract plus the consequences for failing to comply with them will be agreed by both parties and their solicitors.

Now most honest people believe the only way they'll ever find themselves being prosecuted in a court of law is if they somehow break the law, unfortunately this couldn't be further from the truth.

There is only one legally binding contract that people are encouraged to sign without any legal advice, instead they must rely on either good fortune or death to see them through to the end of it. Have you guessed what it is yet? It's the one and only "till death do you part contract" i.e. MARRIAGE.

How are we allowed sign such a contract? A contract that has no terms and conditions, no termination clause, and is signed while both parties are under the influence of mind altering chemicals.

You may already have one of these contracts or you could be in the process of acquiring one. You could also be in the less fortunate position of trying to terminate one of these "eternal contracts" and you're just now discovering that "ignorance" is no defence.

Ignorant you were signing a legal document.

Ignorant of how difficult it is to live with a woman who's not your mother.

Ignorant that 25% of marriages eventually fail, and of the emotional and financial implications of such a failure.

Did you ever wonder who benefits from the lack of legal advice you receive prior to the signing of an eternal marriage contract! Well it certainly isn't the "gob shite" standing on the altar, dressed in a hired tuxedo, waiting to sign it.

"That shouldn't be required"

"INDEPENDENCE"

For generations men have fought and died for their independence, but unfortunately today's generation of "new men", seem to be willing to give up theirs, without the slightest whimper. You know the type of guy I'm talking about? He meets a girl and all of a sudden he's convinced that they must move in together and "bobs your uncle" his whole life changes in a matter of months.

These poor guys, often don't notice the subtle changes that are taking place, as they struggle to conform to the rules of co-habitation. These rules (unknown to him of course) were drafted for only one reason, and that's to drastically reduce all the free time he wastes! on such trivial pursuits as golf, soccer, beer or god forbid, women!

But don't worry, I'm sure you don't fit the description of a new man! Or do you?

Try remembering back to the time when you and your mates were able to "come" and go as you pleased, watch what you wanted on TV, date different women and have a few beers anytime you liked.

Why has everything changed? What compensation did you receive for all the "slight re-adjustments" you've made to your life?

Do you have a more exciting sex life, more money to spend, freshly cooked meals on your return from a hard days work, your clothes washed and pressed, a kind ear to listen to your troubles or is it just more requests on your ever decreasing spare time?

Surely you have a few plans of your own, or maybe you're happy allowing somebody else plan your life for you.

If you're in any doubt about whose plans you're following, this is a transcript of some advice given to women by their mothers on their twenty first birthdays.

"After you commence any co-habitation arrangement with a member of the opposite sex it's vital to immediately start reducing his sporting activity, his alcohol consumption and most important of all, the time he spends with his "so called" friends.

This process can have dramatic effects on your partners self-esteem. So to help prevent your "new man" from suffering any adverse reaction to all this change, his immediate enforced introduction to activities such as D.I.Y., cooking, cleaning, gardening and eventually child minding is highly recommended".

Don't say you weren't warned!

"Whose life is it anyway?"

"HAPPINESS"

Men are constantly complaining about how difficult it is to make women happy. No matter how hard they try to create the feelings of everlasting happiness, it seems to disappear just as fast as it was created. Did you ever wonder who came up with the word "happiness"? I'm asking you this question because it seems most people are totally preoccupied with finding true happiness. We talk about it constantly "if you're not happy don't do it" or "she's never happy" or "whatever makes you happy" also there's the "but? Is he/she really happy" this only applies to very successful people with loads of money.

Did you ever stop and ask yourself exactly what the word happiness means and when will you know you're truly happy.

Does it take something "bad" to happen for you to realise that you were previously very "happy", or vice versa does something "good", have to happen before you realise that you were previously very "unhappy".

What if we're really happy all the time? But we've become so complacent and greedy that we just don't realise it anymore.

From today say you stopped calling the word "happiness" and instead substituted it with the word "contentment". What do you think would happen? Could this simple stroke of a pen end your fruitless search for the holy grail of "happiness", as suddenly you'd be totally content.

Imagine the immediate benefits! Such as "contented women"... Dream on.....

"Contentment"

"EXPECTATIONS"

To enable you understand how people's expectations can change after they get married, we decided to ask various couples attending a pre-marriage course to answer some simple questions. Below is a list of the questions we asked each couple, accompanied in brackets, by the most common responses we received.

"THE SINGLE MALE"

A} Nights out (beer in local, talk sport, a club and maybe shag)

B} Plays sport (golf, football, two or three times a week)

C} Watch T.V. (soccer, golf,)

D} Good sex (lots of girls, good blowjobs)

E} Nice wife (looks good, not too loud, enhances his life)

F} Good car (BMW, Mercedes}

G} Holidays (ski, golf, sun, women)

H} Nice house (warm and comfortable)

I} Good job (pays all the bills with some leftover)

"THE SINGLE FEMALE"

A} Nights out (drinks too much while out searching for a husband, slag off guys brave enough to chat them up)

B} Plays sport (hockey or basketball at school)

C} Watch T.V. (Eastenders, Coronation St, Sex in the city)

D} Good sex (too drunk to remember)

E} Nice husband (tall, dark, handsome, funny etc)

F} Good car (Peugeot 206, Opel corsa)

G} Holidays (sunny, lots of men i.e. potential husbands}

H} Nice house (will always need updating or replacement)

I} Good job (pays some of the bills)

Three years later, we returned to ask the original participants of the survey the same questions. Below is the original list of questions we asked each couple accompanied by some very interesting changes to their original replies.

"A MARRIED MALE"

A} Nights out (a few pints with mates once a week)

B} Plays sport (golf or football once a week if lucky)

C} Watch T.V. (Eastenders, Coronation St, sky sports if lucky)

D} Good sex (fantasises about when he was single)

E} Nice wife (moody, knows everything)

F} Good car (people carrier and Peugeot 206)

G} Holidays (sunny with wife)

H} Nice house (needs updating or replacement)

I} Good job (more work, less money)

"A MARRIED FEMALE"

A} Nights out (talking about kids, decorating or moving house)

B} Plays sport (wants to learn to play golf)

C} Watch T.V. (Eastenders, Coronation St, Sex in the city, odd match)

D} Good sex (forgets to give blow jobs, remembers everything else}

E} Nice husband (average looking, tries to be funny)

F} Good car (people carrier and Peugeot 206)

G} Holidays (anywhere sunny with husband)

H} Nice house (redecorated but hopefully moving to a new one)

I} Good job (but wants to give it up to mind the kids)

"THE BASTARD AND THE BITCH"

How many times have you heard it said "women love a bastard" or "treat them mean and keep them keen"? Why is it that so many women either fancy or fall in love with complete bastards?

Now I don't mean those cowardly bastards who are "physically or emotionally" violent towards women as this behaviour is totally deplorable from any so called man.

No I'm talking about the guy who doesn't care what the woman in his life thinks, as he's going to do exactly what he pleases and if she doesn't like it she can close the door on her way out.

Do you ever wonder how these guys get away with this so called bad behaviour? Is it because they're great lovers? Are their one liner's really that funny? Do they have lots of money, or is it the selection process that they use the key to their success.

Maybe they only date women who suit their way of life ie women they can control/manipulate, or women who don't require too much maintenance. Occasionally these so called "selfish bastards" maybe required to give a few compliments, or use a bit of emotional blackmail to get their own way, but who cares! as long as they're not hurting anybody, what's the problem?

But hold on a minute! Does the behaviour of this "selfish bastard" remind you of anybody?

Have you not experienced this same type of behaviour

from somebody who searched long and hard to find you? Somebody who also wants everything their own way and who's also partial to dispensing some emotional blackmail.

Figured it out yet? It's the one and only "selfish bitch"! Now can you understand why women love these so called bastards?

The reason is quite simple! We're all more comfortable when we're surrounded by people who think like us and act like us! so who's kidding who?

"It takes one to know one"

Equality my arse!! Why is it when a man talks dirty to a woman its sexual harassment? But when a woman talks dirty to a man, its 4 euro a minute!

"THE NEW WOMAN"

Her arms are gradually becoming shorter, as she no longer carries any heavy loads i.e. shopping, coal or wet washing.

Her cooking abilities are limited to reheating.
For her house cleaning and ironing skills see "the new man"

Her erratic driving skills which until recently were confined to the overtaking lanes of dual carriageways, are now displayed daily at her local golf club.

Her ability to talk for hours and divulge nothing of any interest, has baffled interrogators worldwide.

Her skin tone has changed from pinkie white to a yellowy brown.

She has three hair colours blonde, red or badger i.e. black with a grey stripe.

Her nails are constantly manicured to remove any dirt deposits that might build up while she's out playing golf.

While she loves having a "new man" around to do all the menial chores, when it comes time for the important stuff a good looking rough and ready guy always has a bit more to give! Right girls.

"New for old, now that's a good swap"

"THE NEW MAN"

His shoulders are very muscular due to large amounts of ironing and cleaning he's expected to do.

His back is distinctly arched from continually bending over backwards.

His social outings are limited to monthly meetings of the local community action group.

His Sporting activities are restricted to the local green.

His main sexual activity takes place on the Sunday of a bank holiday weekend.

His eyes are slightly rectangular due to his constant search for stimulation amongst the sports channels.

His orientation skills have improved enormously due to his constant search for home improvement stores, garden centres and takeaway food outlets.

He has developed a greater understanding of women's needs, which will come in very handy if his present partner ever decides to trade him in for somebody a bit more interesting.

"The new "WO" man"

"HEALTH"

You might find this hard to believe but a man's health is every bit as important as a woman's. Unfortunately most men know far more about the problems that affect women's health, than they do about their own.

Major cancer screening programs have been put in place, to assist women in the early detection of breast and cervical cancer. But men still think silence, ignorance and coffins are the best way to deal with the cancers that affect them, such as testicular and prostate cancer. I suppose this is partly the reason women can expect to live longer than men.

A healthy body is essential if you're to have any chance of enjoying the thirty or so years leading up to your retirement, or the fifteen plus years after retirement, that your pension fund manager, insists, are vital you save for, while at the same time recommending that you take out a large life insurance policy just in case they get it wrong.

The body you're given to live out your short life is a superb machine and it's capable of handling tremendous amounts of abuse.

In your twenties and thirties you can eat, drink and smoke to your hearts content, and still retain your feeling of indestructibility.

But as soon as you reach your forties, that indestructible feeling you've had throughout your youth will suddenly disappear, as unfortunately it becomes pay back time.

Now I'm not going to preach to you about ailments such as heart disease, lung cancer, diabetes or liver disease as I'm sure you're well aware of these problems. No what I want to talk about are side effects of over indulgence that you'll never hear mentioned, well not unless you're unfortunate enough to be diagnosed with one by your local doctor

These problems I'm talking about are known in the medical profession as "erectile malfunction" and "prostate cancer", which translate into lay mans terms as "no horn possible without chemicals" and "problems when you piss".

A word of warning to all those young men out there enjoying the fruits of your youth, if you intend reaching your forties with the big head i.e. "the capsule for your brain" still talking to the little head i.e. "the penis", and the little head still able to understand whats being said, it might be a good idea, if you start reducing the amount of abuse you're inflicting on your body, as this might prevent you from being the only one amongst your friends, who ends up with the little head suffering from a case of premature deafness.

Now on to the prostate gland. This little gland\valve is located at the outlet to your "bladder" i.e. the internal bag that stores your pee. The symptoms associated with an unhealthy prostate gland are a severe pain when you pee or that the flow of your pee becomes restricted.

From the age of forty five onwards, it is highly recommended that men get themselves checked for any internal abnormalities with their prostate gland, as unfortunately cancer can develop inside the gland without displaying any of the above symptoms.

Now for some good news. Prostate cancer is completely curable if it's diagnosed on time, so try not dying unnecessarily and go and get checked by your doctor on a regular basis.

I almost forgot! If you're lucky enough to be in the 18-40 age group and you'd like to enter your forties with a full complement of "balls" still in place, it's a good idea if you regularly check "your balls" for any lumps or bumps and immediately report any changes to your doctor, as unfortunately testicular cancer is a young mans disease which mainly affects men in the 18-40 age group.

"If I knew I was going to live this long I would have looked after myself a lot better".

"ITS MADNESS"

Not to love yourself.

Not to take one day at a time.

Not to forgive yourself.

To feel rejection from refusal.

Not to wear sunscreen.

Not to practice safe sex.

To think everybody else has the problem.

To spend your whole life saving for retirement.

To worry what people think of you, while they spend their time worrying what you think of them.

To let others live your life for you.

*"To repeat the same actions
while hoping for a different result"*

"COMMUNICATION"

Did you ever listen to one of these so called "life coaches" and hear their complicated theories on men's inability to understand what women are "really" saying to them.

Let's have a quick look at some of the complicated language women use, and see if we can figure out exactly what's being said.

<u>"You don't love me anymore"</u>?
The life coach says, "She feels unloved. She thinks you love her but she feels slightly insecure. Tell her you love her and she'll be fine.
The truth/ she's pissed off after catching you staring at another woman.

<u>"You're not listening to me"</u>?
 The life coach says, "She thinks you're bored with her. She feels quite sensitive and needs some special attention. You need to empathise with her....
The truth/ you're watching the sports channel again.

<u>"We never go out"</u>?
The life coach says, "She loves doing things with you as you're so entertaining. How about dinner together? Its ages since you ate out.
The truth/ she's just hungry again..

<u>"You're always rushing"</u>
The life coach says, she wants more quality time. You're always on the move, so she needs some reassurance
The truth/ she's your mistress…

We also asked the same life coach to explain exactly what the man below is saying and give some advice on the steps women can take to rectify any problems.

"I want some peace and quite"
The life coach says/ he needs some peace and quite
The advice/ stop talking..

"I'm fine"
 The life coach says/ he's feeling fine
 The advice/ Just stop talking..

"It's no big deal"
The life coach says/ there's no problem
The advice/ Please stop talking

"I've a pain in my arse"
The life coach says/he hasn't any pain
The advice/ For Gods sake, stop talking..

"We need to talk"
The life coach say/Are you sure he's not gay.
The truth/ don't get your hopes up..!

Ladies how can you expect to be understood, when everything you say, means something totally different.

"Keep it simple"

"EQUAL RIGHTS"

During every relationship, one of the most common causes of arguments between couples, is a women's insistence on being treated as the man's equal, which is something I thoroughly agree with. But the problems start arising when women start contradicting themselves, by insisting on being given preferential treatment to the men when it suits them.

If you're unable recall any specific areas of your life where the woman of your dreams, is automatically given preferential treatment, you are probably still happily married to her(see courtroom battles) or else you don't play golf.

Let's take golf as our example! When a man plays golf with a woman for the first time, it doesn't take him long to realise that women are allowed to play golf, using a totally different set rules.

The most obvious difference to the rules being the location of the women's tee boxes, which can be located anywhere between 80 and 150 metres closer to the green than the men's tee boxes.

Women also insist on being allocated five strokes to complete certain holes while men are only allocated four, even though the length of the hole is considerably longer for men.

Then to cap it all, women are awarded handicaps that are so high, it allows them the luxury of never having hit a ball far enough to lose it, which in turn adds greatly to their enjoyment of the game.

These rule changes which were designed specifically to facilitate women, who wish to play golf on "man sized courses", shouldn't concern men too much, as long as they don't reinforce women's belief that they're entitled to preferential treatment over men in other aspects of their life.

Before we finish I have a couple of questions I'd like to ask: 1) Why is it that men have no problem being segregated from women on golf courses but women seem to have a major problem if they're segregated from the men? 2) Why don't groups of lady golfers join together to finance the building of golf courses designed specifically for the needs of Lady golfers? Think of the benefits! The course would only need half the land that's normally required. It could be built on land that's unsuitable for a man's golf course, such as land located on the side of a hill. The tee-box for each hole could be located on top of the hill with the greens at the bottom. There would be no need to install expensive water hazards or bunkers and all the greens could be shaped like your standard saucer "not upturned like the men's", with the hole being located in the centre.

A giant Escalator could then be installed to whisk the women back up the hill after they'd played each hole. Can you imagine the benefits such a golf course would make to the woman's game? Suddenly they'd be able to play the game without the constant distraction of having to look over their shoulders every two minutes to see if they're holding up play for any of the male members plus their handicaps would start to plummet? Now this solution sounds great in theory, until you do some research on the subject, and find there's one major flaw. It unfortunately doesn't take into consideration the amount of women who actually like each other.

"Equal for whom"

"LOVE"

A chance meeting brings you both together.

A meeting that changes your life.

A meeting where you communicate on a different level.

They are interesting.

They are thoughtful.

They make you laugh.

They may make you cry.

They turn sex into love making.

They convert loneliness into companionship.

Separation is like an eternity.

They feel your hurt.

Love is precious.

Never become complacent about love.

"Is a wonderful thing"

"MR MONOGAMY"

The main reason for a man's presence on earth is procreation i.e. to strengthen the species by impregnating as many women as possible. Not as is so often the case, to help weaken it, by being afraid to say the word no.

In the bible it's written, "thou shalt not covet thy neighbour's wife"! Which might give those adventurous types who like to participate in the odd bit of wife swapping a little cause for concern, but for the rest of mankind its just sound advice. Now before you start jumping to conclusions and imagine "wife swapping" might somehow be the answer to all your prayers, like all good ideas it has its drawbacks. Firstly you must be married to be allowed to participate in the swapping process and secondly it is only a temporary arrangement! Now I'm all for having rules and trying to live by them, and I also except that chasing after your neighbours wife does have its down side, especially if you happen to catch her and her husband finds out.

But what I don't agree with is, the women's abstinence movement being allowed to turn simple words of advice like! "Thou shalt not covet thy neighbour's wife" into rules that must be adhered to. As this has the effect of turning honest decent family men, whose only crime in life was failing to suppress a natural urge to procreate, into men who are branded as cheats and liars.

So maybe it's about time women started to cut men some slack for the occasional slip they make along the road to total abstinence, as unfortunately men just can't do "abstinence" the way women do.

"St Peter"

"EMOTIONAL CONTROL"

Are you one of those unlucky guys whose partner is incapable of accepting the blame for any of their actions? Are you constantly bombarded with emotional blackmail to make you feel guilty for her selfishness?

WELL DON'T WORRY HELP IS ON ITS WAY!!

While conducting another of my in-depth surveys into men suffering from emotional blackmail:
I asked each man for two words which could be used to defend themselves against the kind of "ball busting" listed below:

"You would if you loved me".

"You're so selfish".

"You never do anything to help me".. Etc.

The men we surveyed voted unanimously for the use of the words "YOU'RE RIGHT" - as they felt these two words instantly acknowledge the wisdom of their persecutors statement while relieving them of the any need to justify their reply.

"PEOPLE PLEASING"

Lots of people waste so much time pandering to the needs of individuals who really don't deserve it. You know the type? They're never happy no matter what you do for them.

The people I'm referring to are the "takers" of this world, those individuals who prey on people who are inflicted with a need to constantly give. These kind and caring people i.e. "the givers" are gradually pressurised by some skilful use of emotional blackmail, into catering for the "takers" every need.

When a "giver" initially gets involved with a "taker" their initial feelings are ones of elation as their need to give is constantly satisfied by the "takers" never ending demands. This feeling of elation may soon change to feelings of anger and resentment, as they gradually realise a "takers" needs are impossible to satisfy.

This cycle of abuse will continue until the giver either passes away or becomes desperate enough to utter the word "no".This word provokes tremendous anger in "takers" as the only thing a "taker" is unable to take, is responsibility for their selfishness. Once you mention the word "no" to a "taker", they can become totally irrational, and start imagining that it's the "giver" whose mean and selfish one, for rejecting their demands.

The"taker" may become so upset at what they perceive is the "givers" selfishness, that they immediately try to force the "giver" into giving once more. But this time it's the givers "understanding" that the "taker" wants.

So if you're not too confused by now and you feel your partner fits the description of a "taker", try saying "no" to some of their selfish demands, you just might get lucky and they'll disappear out of your life or at the very least realise you're alive.

A taker: is a person who uses their partner's time, money, understanding and confidence for their own selfish needs.

A giver: enables that same self centred insecure bully to function.

"Give and take"

"THE POINTS SYSTEM"

I hope you realise that long before any government decided to issue points on your driving licence for motor offences, women were using a similar system to allocate points to their partners, depending on the amount of chores they complete.

Once you understand how women allocate these points, you'll never again have to utter those immortal words "she's never bleed'n happy, no matter what I do".

It's quite simple! All you have to remember while doing the chores is that your partner will automatically allocate you one point for every chore you successfully complete. Example: if you open a door, buy flowers, mind the kids, remember her birthday, make her a cup of coffee, do some painting etc, she will automatically add one point to the credit side of her brain, which can be traded in by you for a game of golf, a few pints with your mates or maybe an unplanned shag.

The main problem with this system arises when you try earning extra points by doing something extravagant. It's not too unreasonable to think, that something like updating her car or buying a new conservatory, might gain you some precious extra points, that can be traded in at a later date for a weekend away with your mates.

In a normal trading environment this would be seen as a fair trade, but unfortunately a woman's brain is not programmed for fair trade. It doesn't matter how much you spend or how hard you work every chore is allocated only one point.

You're probably thinking this system isn't very fair and you're probably right. But there's another problem with it and it's this. When you eventually get to "trade in" the points you've worked so hard to collect they disappear extremely quick. The reason for this is as follows, if you do anything that remotely looks like you're enjoying yourself i.e. drinking with your mates, playing sport or staying out after normal curfew, she will immediately start deducting five of your hard earned points for each of the rules you break. As you can imagine it doesn't take very long for you to use up all your hard earned credit.

I hope this, in some small way helps to explain why it's virtually impossible to make any woman happy for too long. So the next time you feel like splashing out on some expensive item for the love of your life, in the vain hope that she'll really appreciate your efforts, you might find it just as effective and a lot less expensive to head out into the kitchen and make her a nice cup of coffee!

"THEY'RE ALL THE SAME"

Unless you've been extremely lucky. There comes a time in most men's personal relationships, when a strange sense of "deja vous" comes over them. Suddenly they realise that their present partner has started making the same "old complaints" as "all" their previous partners used to make.

It gradually starts to dawn on them that every one of these women seemed to want exactly the same things. It starts off with the engagement, moves as quickly as possible on to marriage and eventually ends with the total control of your everyday life.

But how does this continually happen? We're not stupid are we? Surely we've learned something from all our previous relationships. Ah stop worrying the answer is quite simple.

Women discovered a long time ago that men rely heavily on appearances when they're choosing a long term partner. They know if they can alter their appearance even slightly, either by some clever use of clothes, make up, or in the more extreme cases cosmetic surgery, they can easily disguise the fact that all their brains are cloned from the one source.

However this illusion doesn't come cheap and it becomes increasingly more expensive to maintain as each year passes. So you can see it's vital that women find somebody interested enough in their present appearance that they would be prepared to finance its future upkeep. So with desperation starting to set in, it suddenly dawns on them, that men might actually be good for something. Thus they head out in search of a man who's foolish enough to take them at "face value". And doesn't he get a very expensive surprise.

"High maintenance"

THE "NEW CAR" VIRUS

So you have been married for some years. You feel fantastic! Your life couldn't be better! But suddenly you're struck down by overwhelming feelings of boredom. What on earth has happened? Why are you feeling this way? Are you working too hard? Maybe it's a mid life crises? Or are have you contracted the "new car" virus.

The "new car" virus is no laughing matter as it strikes both married men and those in long term relationships. The first signs of the infection are an overwhelming feeling of boredom. This usually results in the infected person continually arguing with their wife or partner as he feels it's her who's responsible for his constant boredom. These arguments gradually become so heated that the infected person can suddenly, decide that he's had enough of married life and he wants out.

Within days he leaves his house, his wife and possibly a few children, before handing his entire emotional and financial future over to solicitors, a course of action that quickly rids him of any feelings of boredom, then after years of expensive litigation and emotional turmoil he finally gets what he's always wanted, and that's his freedom.

Now what does he do?

Does he head off into the sunset to enjoy his new found freedom? I'd like to think so, but unfortunately the "new car" virus isn't finished with him yet.

Just as he's ready to get his life back in order, disaster strikes! And it comes in the form of a secondary infection.

This secondary infection alters the part of the brain that controls logic. This has a dramatic effect on men who suffer a relapse, as it turns cautious careful individuals into what psychologists describe as "optimistic masochists".

These optimistic masochists behave very strangely. They suddenly forget all the pain and suffering they've endured to enable them to reclaim their new found freedom and become convinced that the only path to true happiness, is when they are firmly entrenched in another long term relationship.

So off they head with the same old criteria they used to choose their previous partner i.e. looks, bodywork and performance.

Initially he's very successful using this criteria, as he doesn't need to waste precious time searching for women who are intellectually compatible.

But sadly! After years of frustration trying to find the perfect look and body shape, it finally dawns on him, while looks and body shape are great on short trips, its comfort and reliability that matter on a long journey.

"Everything has its price"

"DIFFERENCES"

Men need space for the same reason women need companionship.

Men require appreciation, women reassurance.

A women's infidelity is painful to a man due to the sexual connection involved. A man's infidelity is painful to a woman due to the emotional connection involved.

Women want empathy, men require solutions.

Women live longer.

Women wonder what men are thinking while men are wondering about the sports results.

Men rationalise, women exaggerate.

"DIFFERENCES 2"

Men hate to be pitied, women insist on it.

Men talk about problems they need solved while women talk about problems they already have.

Men want to feel needed while women need to feel cherished.

Women like change, unfortunately men don't.

Women love romance, men love sky sports.

There's one thing men and women will never understand and that's each other.

Women worry until they get married, men don't start till afterwards.

Men cry at sporting events, women cry about everything else.

"A woman marries a man expecting him to change, but he doesn't, a man marries a woman expecting that she won't change and she does".

"WEIGHT WATCHERS"

Most women these days seem totally obsessed with loosing weight.

If it's not for their compulsion to walk five miles a day, or go to the gym seven days a week for the six weeks leading up to any weddings or sun holidays, it's their insistence on participating in the special k, two week "drop a jean size" challenge i.e. they'll eat a bowl of special k for breakfast and a bowl of special k for lunch. This is followed by their normal dinner, consisting of all the food they didn't eat at breakfast and lunch"! And hey presto, two weeks later they'll have miraculously dropped a jean size.

But it doesn't stop there! If for any reason there's the slightest doubt in their mind that they didn't complete the challenge successfully i.e. they find themselves having to lie on the flat of their back to pull on their new jeans, they'll immediately move to plan B.

This plan will only allow the participants to buy food with low-fat or diet written on the packaging, and once it's initiated, out will go all the full cream milk and black forest gateaux and in will come the diet cheese cake and low fat crisps.

Then before too long there's diet coke being mixed with the bacardi, and all the late night snacks will no longer come covered in curry sauce. Now if that's not dedication I don't know what is?

So now your aware of the kind of effort that's goes into keeping women slim and trim, do you not feel a slight bit guilty, having all that relaxed muscle, hanging over your waist band?

Or are you one of those ingenious men who never diets or exercises but can still claim to have a 38 inch waist.

O.k.! Your waist may have moved up under your chin, or it might have dropped down to just below your hips. But who cares? As long as you can solve either of these problems with a little help from a tailor or a very strong belt.

"INFIDELITY"

How many men can put their hand on their heart and swear to their almighty god, they've never been unfaithful to their partner.

Some surveys might produce a figure of about 60%. An educated guess might be closer to 40%, but if the men involved were not required to back up their claims with results from a lie detector test that figure would almost certainly decrease to 10%.

If you believe the figures from above, then 40% of married men probably strayed at one time or other, 60% of married men definitely strayed, but the true figure will never be known as they will all deny straying, if they're given the chance.

There are generally only two opportunities men get to be unfaithful to their partners. The first is while they are away with their mates on a short break and the second is while attending their annual Christmas party.

Most women are well aware of the temptations faced by men at these events, and it can cause them a great deal of necessary worry in the days or weeks leading up to such an event.

"Look I know you've never strayed on your partner, so will you stop worrying, this isn't about you, and that feeling of guilt you have at the moment was triggered by distant memory, and I'm sure it will pass as soon as you turn to the next page"

Sorry about that! Just making sure nobody has started to panic.

Now where was I!

Oh yes, the reason for all this "necessary worry" is quite simple.

Unlike the average woman, men are pre-programmed from birth to do everything in their power to keep the species strong i.e. to procreate, otherwise known as "shagging as many different women as possible".

This "cross" of procreation that men are forced to carry, is a major cause for concern amongst women, as they're constantly on their guard for any subtle changes to their partner's behaviour, changes that might indicate a dangerously high hormone level which left untreated could force their partner into a reckless act of procreation .i.e. a one night stand.

So lads if you're ever forced into a reckless act of procreation i.e. "a one night stand that requires some coyote treatment", try not being too hard on yourselves, as how can you hold yourself responsible for your genetic make-up or your partner's inability to spot the danger signs.

A man out shopping happens to notice a blonde lady staring at him.
She waves over at him, and he reply's sorry but do I know you?
She says I think you're the father of one of my children! The man casts his mind back to the one and only time he was ever unfaithful. He then asks her, if she's the stripper from his stag party that he shagged over the pool table, while her friend stuck a cucumber up his arse. No she replies I'm your son's English teacher.

"PLAYING THE GAME"

Is this what its all about at the end of the day, just learning to play the game? You start out with all these romantic ideas about life with a new partner and finish up being bored out of your brains with routine.

You get the odd chance to get away with your friends, where you hopefully, meet somebody of the opposite sex, and engage in some harmless flirtation which might just end in a good shag, but as nobody ever finds out what's the big deal.

Then it's back home feeling revived. You might feel slightly guilty about your little indiscretion, so your partner gets the added benefit of a more attentive you, well for a week or so, or at least until the guilt wears off, whichever comes first. Then it's back to your normal boring routine which is only punctuated by the odd game of golf or a few beers with your friends, where the main topic of conversation is the little indiscretions you had on previous holidays or planning the location of the next one.

Really girls! Is this any way to treat the man in your life…?

An Englishman, Irishman and a Scotsman arrive at the gates of heaven. Peter asks each of the men, if they were ever unfaithful to their wives. The Englishman replies no and he's awarded a rolls royce to drive around heaven. The Scotsman says he was unfaithful twice and Peter awards him a B.MW to drive around heaven. When it comes to the Irishman's turn, he tells Peter that he was unfaithful every chance he got. So Peter awards him a motor cycle to drive around heaven. So all three head out for their first look around heaven, after a while the Irishman comes across the Englishman's car parked in a lay-by, with the Englishman sitting inside crying. The Irishman decides to tap on the window to ask him why he's crying. The Englishman opens the window and tells the Irishman, that he's just seen his wife pass-by, cycling a bicycle!

"Who's playing who"

A guilty feeling can be triggered by something as serious as "failing to buy your round at the bar" or as trivial as "having an affair with your partners best friend".

These self inflicted feelings are about as useful as "an ashtray on a motorbike".

Imagine for a moment, that you're having regular "deep and meaningful" secret conversations with your partner's best friend, when suddenly you get an overwhelming feeling of guilt. What should you do?

Tell your partner!

Stop the conversations!

Blame the guilty feelings on your catholic up-bringing!

Convert to Catholicism! As being a catholic is a good excuse.

Or tell nobody!

Telling your partner! This will have the immediate effect of ridding you of any "imaginary pain" you might be feeling due to the onset of the guilt, but beware! Your inability to suffer this "imaginary pain" in silence may eventually cause you a great deal of "real pain".

Stopping the conversations! A gradual reduction in such conversations is highly recommended, as any "sudden" stoppage could leave your partners best friend with far too much to say.

Blaming Religion! Putting the blame on your religious up-bringing, is a marvellous way to justify your actions.

Changing religion! This can be a terrific distraction as you wait for your feelings of guilt to subside.

Tell nobody! This is the safest long term solution to any feeling of guilt, because once you've learned to live with the "imaginary pain" involved, you'll be free to "come" and go as you please!

As long as you don't get caught that is....

It is so simple to be wise, just think of something stupid to say and then don't say it.

"Catholic"

"THE LIAR"

A major survey on lying, has concluded that men and women tell lies as often as each other, the only difference being the type of lies they like to tell.

It seems a woman will tell lies to provoke an argument about something she wants to talk about or when she's trying to make somebody feel good. But a man tells lies to make himself look good or to avoid arguments.

There are many different kinds of liars. On the one hand you've the professional liars, whose occupations range from politicians to used car salesmen. While on the other you've got the opportunistic liars who mainly confine their lying to nights out with the boys.

Now, it's not difficult to recognise a professional liar as they normally dress up before telling lies. Some professional liars dress up in a wig and gown to tell theirs, while others just need a suit with a rosette pinned to the lapel, before they're comfortable enough to go door to door peddling their lies and broken promises.

But in order to see the opportunistic liar in action, you either need to be female or the opportunist's best friend. You see the opportunist's lying strategy is based solely on restricting the amount of information he divulges, which helps him to reduce his chances of being caught lying, as he is not required to remember large amounts of useless information.

Let's take Peter as our example.

Peter is in a long term relationship with Mary.

One night while he's out with the boy's Peter meets a girl he fancies called Linda. During their conversation Linda asks Peter if he's married, to which Peter immediately answers "no". Four hours later as Peter is climbing out of Linda's bed to rush home to Mary, Linda asks, "where are you rushing off to", Peter immediately divulges the fact that he's in a long term relationship and must get home. Linda responds by asking Peter why he never told her about this, Peter continues to pulls up his trousers, put on his jacket, check his pockets for his phone, keys and money before he replies "you only asked me was I married". So Peter heads home delighted with the fact that he never told Linda any lies. Mary is in bed fast asleep and none the wiser, while poor Linda is left wondering if she'll ever meet an honest man, who doesn't need to rush home halfway through their first night together.

Below are listed four well known lies. Three of them are mainly used by men, with the fourth being mainly used by women.

> (1) No I wasn't drinking
> (2) You're the best ever
> (3) I'll pull out
> (4) I'll give you a call

If you've any trouble spotting the odd one out, try putting the words "How was I" before each one and see if that will help.

"Needs the gullible"

You're probably looking at the heading from above and wondering to yourself, what on earth is P.D.A?

If you're confused about the "real" meaning of these three letters, you can stop worrying, as all is about to be revealed.

This may come as a shock to most women, but the two main reasons men are either unwilling or unable to indulge in the odd P.D.A. are firstly, personal security and secondly, the fact that men's only other experience of a P.D.A. is gleaned from the mobile internet connectors that "some?"? men use to access "internet porn sites" from the privacy of the men's room i.e. the "Personal Digital Assistant"!

When in fact the "real" meaning of the letters P.D.A., as interpreted by women that it's your simple run of the mill "Public Display of Affection".

To enable women to better understand the security implications of a Public Display of Affection, I've listed below the four main P.D.A's, accompanied by various explanations as to why men find them so dangerous to perform.

Holding hands. Every man knows this can be extremely dangerous. The reason it's so dangerous is personal security. It's perfectly safe to hold hands on a desert island as there's very little chance of a surprise attack from "bag snatchers" or "unwanted" admirers, but unfortunately the same can't be said about the main streets of most major towns or cities.

Placing an arm around your partner's waist. This could tempt a "bag snatcher" into attempting an opportunist strike, due to the hands of both parties being severely restricted

Kissing in public. Unfortunately this has the potential of attracting the attention of "unwanted" admirers.

Pushing a baby's pram one handed. This allows men to have one hand free to fend off any potential "baby snatchers" or to catch anything the baby happens to throw at him.

So the next time your partner becomes annoyed at your failure to display your "undoubted" affection towards her, to the general public, ask her one simple question. Does she feel safe in your presence?

If the answer is yes, just smile! Tap her on the arse (- a P.D.A that allows you to leave both hands free -) and congratulate yourself on a job well done.

"Are not for the faint hearted"

"P.M.S"

This must be the greatest public relations coup ever achieved by women. Can you think of any other medical condition, which allows the sufferer a carte blanche excuse to be in bad humour or totally irrational any time they want, and for as long as they want, while at the same time expecting the focus of these irrational ranting i.e. "the man in their life" to show them some kindness and understanding.

Would it not be more appropriate for sufferers of such a medical condition to apologise for all the trouble their temperamental behaviour causes?

Imagine for a moment, if doctors suddenly discovered that men also suffered from a mood altering complaint, one which surpassed the mood altering capabilities of P.M.S.. A complaint doctors called P.I.S "Pre Intercourse Syndrome", which must be treated regularly to prevent it from building up in a man's body causing him to behave totally irrationally.

Can you imagine the sympathy and understanding men would get for their "P.I.S" and the effort that would be made to ease their suffering?

So the next time you're informed that "P.M.S" is the reason the woman in your life is in such a shitty humour, by all means be compassionate, then inform her of your good news. At long last doctors have discovered the reason for men's infrequent bad humours and with some regular help from herself, your frowns will be gone forever..... dream on.....

"Whose problem is it anyway?"

"MEMORY"

This is definitely one area where women win hands down. Has your partner ever reminded you of some "horrendous deed", that you supposedly carried out against her, at a certain time, on a certain date, some three years previously.

This incredible ability to instantly recall all their partners past indiscretions, is due mainly to the selection process, women use to filter information.

This process which is commonly known as "selective memory", only enables women to store information that they deem useful to themselves. This might help to explain women's inability to recall anything positive that their partner might do for them, or any of the promises that she makes to him regarding her overspending or their sex life.

So lads the next time your partner reminds you of some long past indiscretion, try not getting too upset, as like most things she reminds you of, you will probably have forgotten all about it by the end of the day, but you can be rest assured the woman of your dreams certainly won't.

"The inability to forget is infinitely more devastating, than the inability to remember"

"MID-LIFE"

You're forty, you're in good health, all your children are working, you've just paid off your mortgage and your sitting watching television in the comfort of your own sitting room, when suddenly your partner of 20 years turns into a complete stranger.

Imagine, somebody you've loved for 20 years becoming a complete stranger in a matter of minutes.

How could this possibly happen? Did you eat a dodgy beef burger in your youth? Perhaps you're the first person to suffer from instantaneous Alzheimer's disease. Or maybe your partner has just uttered those immortal words "I don't love you anymore".

To check if you're suffering from either of the first two scenarios you'll need to contact your local doctor.

On the other hand, if you're a vegetarian and you haven't suddenly started to eat fillet steak for your dinner, I'd be more inclined to go with the "I need some space i.e. I don't love you anymore scenario.

Once you're certain that your partner has taken enough time to study the implications of their decision and they still remain adamant that they want to terminate the relationship, it won't do any harm to start looking at the options that are left open to you.

The first option open to you is mediation!
It's important to remember, mediation can only work if both parties are prepared to put aside their differences, listen to the counsellors advice, accept some criticism and implement new ways of communicating with each other.

The second option is blame and self pity!
Self pity is acceptable in the short term, as everybody needs time to grieve the ending of a relationship. But blaming your now ex-partner for its failure, will only prolong your pain and unhappiness.

The third option is not to accept what your partner is telling you!
This might keep you together in the short term, but as the days pass and the level of questioning grows in intensity, your partners respect for you might diminish to the point where the word hate is used far more frequently than the word love.

The fourth option is forgiveness!
Forgiving both yourself and your partner will take immense courage, but try keeping in mind your partner didn't fall in love with you, with the intention of falling out of love at a later date. Unfortunately sometimes it just happens that way.

Your fifth option is to pick up the pieces and move on!
Most people find this option difficult and frightening. Trying to reinvent yourself while your mind longs for the stability of a past relationship is tremendously difficult. But if you remain patient and give yourself some time, your partner's sudden change of heart, while extremely painful to you at the time, may just be the start of a new beginning.

And last but by no means least, is option number six!
This is for people who don't want to waste time on options 1-5. As they believe the best way to get over somebody, is to get somebody new straight back under them.

"Crises"

"MARRIAGE GUIDANCE"

When most of us decide to get married, it's usually without the slightest thought of what will happen if the marriage ever fails. Most sane people decide to get married with the sole intention of staying married as you'd want to be a complete lunatic to get married with the intention of separating at a later date.

If you believe that your partner's intentions were completely honourable when you got married, then it stands to reason that the sad demise of your marriage is not their sole responsibility.

So what about some counselling? I know what you're thinking, what good is counselling when you already know who has the problem! and it's certainly not you? A small word of advice! Before deciding to finish any relationship, (especially one where children are involved)it makes both emotional and financial sense for both of you to find a suitably qualified person to sit down and listen to your grievances, as depending on family and friends or your local pub counsellors for guidance, can have tragic consequences, as no matter how good you "think" their advice seems to be, it will always be unreliable. The reason for this is simple: Your family and friends base their advice on only your side of the story as they're unable to access the other side, which is your partner's, with the truth lying somewhere in between.

If you are still intent on betting your entire emotional and financial future on the advice of friends that's fine by me but your children might prefer if you dealt with professionals only.

Unfortunately, any counselling you receive may only confirm what you already know, that separation is the best course of action for both of you.

On the other hand you might be surprised to find a compromise solution to your grievances, but whatever happens, at least you'll be talking to each other even if it's only with the help of a professional counsellor.

But if you're still adamant that talking is a waste of time and revenge is what you desire, then there's always the family "injustice" court.

Now instead of talking to each other, you get to employ your very own teams of parasites, sorry I mean solicitors, to do all your talking for you.

These parasites "solicitors" will only be too delighted to help you gain your expensive revenge. A word of warning though, once you get parasites involved, there's no chance of a fair solution, as parasites need your anger and bitterness to feed themselves.

Eventually, when your painful and costly battle finally ends, who is left to pick up the pieces? Certainly not your expensive team of parasites, no! The only people left are yourself, your now former partner and your children.

So before you decide to give large amounts of your hard earned money to some soulless parasite, why not give yourself and your children a chance. Go and get yourself a counsellor who's trained to deal with relationship problems and go talk to them or better still *try listening!*

"Talk is cheaper"

"JUST PASSING THROUGH"

~ Your dreams shouldn't be kept waiting, as tomorrow is promised to nobody.

~ Tell the people you love, exactly that.

~ Realise you own mortality.

~ Do the things you fear.

~ Don't be taken prisoner by money.

~ Help those less fortunate.

~ Smile more.

~ Count your blessings, except your troubles, and waste no time on regrets.

~ Make provision for your future while allowing for change and disappointment.

~ Forgive yourself for past mistakes and forgive others theirs.

~ Enjoy everyday as if it were your last, as one day you'll be delighted you did.

~ Opinions are like arseholes, everybody seems to have one.

"So enjoy it"

"WATER-WORKS"

How many times have you allowed two small droplets of water to completely alter the outcome of an argument? You know what I mean. You're in the middle of some fierce negotiations with your partner, which by all accounts you're winning, when suddenly, your partner decides it time to introduce her main negotiation skill i.e. a sudden discharge of water from each eye.

Initially women used this discharge of water to clean away excess mascara from their eyes, until one day a woman noticed the dramatic effect her eye cleansing was having on her partner, as it seemed to be able to distract him from watching sky sports. Armed with this discovery she began to train herself to discharge water from her eyes at the slightest sign of confrontation, as she realised if it could distract her partner from sky sports it would certainly distract him from the truth.

To try and help men differentiate between eye cleansing and manipulation, we have developed a simple test.If you happen to notice water streaming from your partners eyes and it's contaminated with mascara, you can relax, as this is only eyewash. If on the other hand the water discharged is clear in colour and is not accompanied by a major tragic event ("I'm talking life and death here and not just your inability to read her mind") be very careful, as these tiny trickles of water are capable of altering decisions and hiding the truth.

"Tears for a clown"

"COURTROOM BATTLES"

This is a brief word of warning to those men out there who have never broken any laws, yet through the unfortunate failure of their marriage will soon find themselves fighting a bitter divorce or child custody battle against their former partner and her expensive legal team down in the local family "injustice" court.

It's extremely important that you prepare yourself thoroughly before entering any family law court and listed below is some general information on family law court procedures that may be of some help to you, as you prepare yourself to be shafted.

All family "injustice" cases revolve around home ownership, money and child custody and have absolutely nothing to do with what's fair, because all the decisions made by the court are based solely on what's best for your children and the children's mothers, so try not to take them too personally. You may enter the court with your family home, twenty four hour access to your children and some disposable income, and through no fault of your own leave the exact same court with no family home, access to your children being controlled by a very bitter ex partner and every penny you earn being spent on maintaining your previous life and renting a room in which to survive in.

As you can imagine the outcome of these cases can have a devastating effect on the personal lives of the men involved, and for this reason I've compiled a list of the various options can men take to help them deal with the devastation that's caused by the decisions of the injustice courts. The first and certainly most successful option is to quickly develop your sense of humour. The second option is one I wouldn't recommend as it's used mainly by men who feel their life has become completely hopeless! Why they feel so hopeless is still a mystery, as unfortunately none of the men who take this option live to tell their tale. The third option is to try and recall any conversations you've had with men who previously experienced the family injustice system. Men you probably dismissed as male chauvinist pigs i.e. women haters, men that you can now draw comfort from as you suddenly realise that you're not the first man to be treated so unfairly by the family injustice courts, it just feels that way.

Scared yet? Well you should be! Or are you smug enough to believe it will never happen to you, as your wife or partner actually really loves you.

I will let you in on a secret regarding men and women and the emotional changes that take place when a marriage / relationship finally ends.

Throughout most men's marriages they are constantly badgered by their wives to "get in touch" with their emotions, as their wives feel emotionally neglected.

But after the marriage ends a strange thing happens. Suddenly there's a complete role reversal. Men suddenly become emotional i.e. god love her, she doesn't mean it, I know she'll do what's best.

As the man struggles to understand all these new emotions, the woman he feels so sorry for starts becoming totally unemotional.

She now decides to "shaft the bastard" and proceeds with the help of a few well paid parasites i.e. solicitors to go after everything she believes is "rightfully hers" which translates legally in to "absolutely everything".

Now you may find the above views slightly unbalanced, as I never mentioned the "genuine bastards", ie those men who don't take responsibility for their actions, and instead, decide to blame their ex partner and everybody else while abandoning their children both emotionally and financially to live out their lives in denial. On the other hand to be judged as if you're a complete bastard for no other reason than being a male is equally unbalanced.

Be careful out there!

"No Winners"

"BUNNY BOILER SYNDROME"

Description of sufferers - women and guy's who act like women.

Cause - broken relationship.

Why - selfishness, insecurity.

Symptoms - delusional, self pitying.

Effects - everybody especially children.

Duration - can last a lifetime.

Benefits - solicitors.

Results - constant unhappiness.

Only known prevention - staying single.

Cure - their former partners demise.

Identification - become irrational when they hear the word "no".

Survival tips - being deaf helps but certainly never look happy.

"It's always someone else's fault"

"WORRY"

This really is the piss taker in life as it seems most of what we worry about never seems to happen, while events we never think about jump up and bite us on the arse.

If this was a multiple choice question and I asked you to list what's most important to worry about, what would be your answer.

> Would you worry more about
> - money,
> - health,
> - Children,
> - work,
> - living,
> - dying
> - or all of the above?

Now the second question I wish to ask you is this. Can you tell me what you shouldn't worry about? If you're worried about the answer to this question I'll give you a hint: try money, health, children, work, living, dying etc.

So try not losing too much sleep worrying over things that might just end up being blessings in disguise.

"Why"

"SELF HELP BOOKS"

You can find these books on the shelves of all good bookstores. These books claim they can "Fix your life"? and cover a wide range of topics such as:

Women who love too much.
Women who love too little.
Find a husband.
Get over a husband.
Going on a date.
Men are from space and women are spacers.
How to loose weight.
How to gain weight.
Good sex.
Bad sex.
Make more money.
Feel the fear.
Get over your fear? Etc

If you ever had reason to read any self help books, you were probably looking for some "quick fix" solution to what you felt at the time was a major problem in your life.

These books are packed full of positive information for people who suffer from the "why me" or "why now" school of thought, when it might be more helpful to these people if the writer asked "why not you" and "why not now"?

S.H.Bs always seem to follow the same format, you skip through the pages searching for some sort of "divine insight" from some of the "quick fix" punch

lines"the writer might express about "your problem".
 This all makes great sense while you're reading the book, but unfortunately more often than not, these incredible insights into "your problem" will fade to a distant memory once you've finished reading the book, as with all "quick fix" solutions they are only words on paper until you put them into practice.

You then find yourself back where you started, still dealing with "your problem" the same one you had before you started the book, but now you're armed with some fancy punch lines on how to solve it. This then gives you another chance to burn the ears off your friends, and anybody else who's prepared to listen long enough to more of your unwanted theories on how to solve "your" problems.

What does the words "self help" mean, does it not mean exactly that i.e. Help yourself.

 Maybe there's no great mystery to this "self help" craze and people are only looking for easy solutions, the type of solution which allows them to blame other people for their problems, and doesn't require them getting off their lazy arses to sort out "their own" problems.

While trying not to sound too uncaring regarding how serious any of the problems you may or may not encounter in life might be, always remember that life is difficult for everybody and that includes you, your family, your friends and that stranger who just walked past your window. Problems mainly arrive unannounced or wearing some type of disguise and most of these problems will pass in time, unfortunately only to make room for some new ones.

A famous publisher once commented on "self help books" "if anybody ever writes a self help book that actually works, it will close us all down". So why not try a new approach to your problems? Try getting your hands on a Lego set, build yourself a bridge and get over it.

"I have been through some terrible things in life, some which actually happened"

"RETIREMENT"

When somebody mentions retirement to you, what is the first thing that springs to mind? Is it holidays in the sun, golf or fishing everyday, no money worries, no more early morning traffic jams or could it be the large amounts of money you are being told to save each month in order to fund these activities after you retire.

 Ok by all means plan for your future, but if your plan entails saving all your spare cash so you can eventually use it to somehow rediscover your youth, forget it, as the only feeling you'll get from a plan like this is a feeling of regret.

 Most people spend far too much of their precious time working for the money required to make totally needless purchases while saving what remains for some future purchases they may never get to make.

"Life is something that happens while you are busy making other plans"

"THE BODY CLOCK"

All men and women have their own personalised body clock, with each clock pre-programmed with a set of alarms calls specifically designed to remind each and every one of us that our lives are slowly ticking away.

The puberty alarm

This alarm goes off when you reach about 10-13 years old. It comes in the form of major body change and has the effect of increasing dramatically the interest that both sexes' take in each other.

When the body clock is satisfied that puberty has been activated, it immediately returns to a silent tick and allows the young boys and girls get on with the serious business of enjoying the fruits of their youth.

The baby alarm

Eventually though, after ticking away unnoticed for a few more years it suddenly activates the second pre-set alarm. This alarm triggers the need in most women to turn their playgrounds into cradles. At the same time as women begin their search for a suitable donor to help with the conversion of the playground into a cradle, the object of their search i.e. the ideal man, gets his own personal alarm call. He starts to notice his hair changing colour and he finds it scattered everywhere i.e. pillow, bathplug and bedroom floor, well everywhere except, where it's needed most i.e. his head.

The mid life crisis alarm.
As the years fly-by, the alarm calls start coming thick and fast. There's the weight alarm which is triggered when women start ignoring their friends reassurances regarding the size of their bums and men are no longer able to see their favourite toy while having a shower. Then it's on to the chemical alarm, where women develop the need for hormones to help them cool down, while men develop a need for Viagra to help them heat up.

 Eventually there comes a time for your clock to stop ticking and hopefully it doesn't come as too much of a surprise.

Enjoy it while it lasts

"THE CHAUVINIST"

Thirty or forty years ago, the main reason men were being classed as male chauvinist pigs was their insistence on chaining their poor unfortunate wives to the kitchen sink. This kind of behaviour may sound a slight bit cruel when you first read about it, but I suppose placing a woman's hands in handcuffs before attaching them to a bed post, might have seemed just as strange to your grandfather.

Fast forward to the twenty first century.

Who calls all the shots these days? Who has all the control? Who "allows" you out and reminds you what time to come back in? Who controls the amount of enjoyment you're allowed and who's never happy?

If the answer to any of the above questions is the women in your life, I now want you to ask yourself the following two questions.

"Why am I allowing my partner live my life for me"

and

"What's in it for me"

If you're not completely happy with the answers to these two questions, I recommend you head down to your local hardware store, buy yourself some chain, and go back to the original arrangement.

"Is rarely understood"

"MORTALITY"

This may come as a surprise to most men, but women have a tendency to live slightly longer. This strange phenomenon gives women one last shot at the single life before they also have to be on their way.

We all travel through life as if we'll be above ground indefinitely which unfortunately couldn't be further from the truth.

While trying not to alarm you, it could all be over by tomorrow, which would be a right pain in the arse after all the plans you have made for the next 30-40 years.

Maybe it's time to stop making excuses and start doing some living. What about fulfiling some of those dreams instead of waiting for some time in the future that may never arrive.

Imagine being told you have only twelve months left above ground what would you do? Carry on as normal or do something completely different.

You're probably saying to yourself what I am supposed to do? Give up work and neglect everything else just incase I might die next year.

That not what I'm saying!

I'm only asking that you keep your own mortality in mind while making all those long term plans, just incase you forget to enjoy the only day you have, which is today.

Spending your time accumulating money is a wonderful pastime once it gives you the freedom to enjoy your life, as the only way money can keep you above ground longer than expected is if you accumulate enough of it to pay for some eternal refrigeration.

"If you don't believe in life after death then you won't even know your dead"

On returning from the doctor, Dave tells his wife he will be dead by dawn of the next day. That night Dave and his wife make love for six hours. Afterwards Dave can't sleep, so he wakes his wife and says darling can we do it one more time. To which she replies "it's alright for you dave, but I've to get up in the morning.

FOOTNOTE

Believe it or not, the male ostrich was written by complete accident. It all started when a friend of mine asked me to write a funny speech for a wedding he was attending. As I began thinking about marriage, it suddenly dawned on me, that anybody who mentions marriage breakdown to the bride or groom, in the weeks leading up to their wedding, is a total cynic. Which I find very strange when you consider 25% of marriages will eventually end in failure.

But I suppose denial on this scale is quite normal, when you consider the amount of people who still have unprotected sex, smoking cigarettes or don't contribute to a pension plan.

Being discouraged from mentioning marriage breakdown or the implications of such is fine, when the society in which the marriage takes place is prepared to help the victims of such a breakdown to rebuild their lives.

But when these victims are being criminalized and forced into a court of law to try and settle their differences, I don't think the occasional mention of marriage breakdown does anybody too much harm.

When I completed the first draft of the male ostrich, I gave it to friends of mine, and asked them for their opinion on what I'd written. The following are some of the comments I received.

Willie and Catherine thought it was good.

Mairead was kind enough to write down some constructive criticism and send it to me.

John thought it was good.

Rachel didn't really like it

My sister Sandra asked me, did I really need the hassle?

Tommy didn't see much point to it.

Emer thought it was o.k., once it wasn't how I really thought.

Deirdre said it was funny, but it shouldn't be taken seriously.

Stephan thought it was good, but more could have been written about men.

Keith and Cass enjoyed it.

Liz said it was good and at least I finished it.

Nuala said, the 90% of men who are complete bastards will defiantly enjoy it, but the remaining 10% would be scared shitless.

Loraine didn't like it and said it didn't contain any of my compassionate nature.

Joan said I sounded like a male chauvinist.

Derek said he enjoyed it, while his Swedish girlfriend lovisa thought it was written by Tony Soprano.

And Last but by no means least is Gerry, he said it was good and that he'd buy 10 copies of it for his friends, I hope he wasn't lying.

After studying the various comments I received, the ones I thought stood out the most were Nuala's and Joan's. The reason I liked Joan's comment so much was its honesty, as it helped confirm my suspicions that any man making negative comments about women, better prepare himself to be branded a male chauvinist.

The other comment that caught my attention was Nuala's. As she believes, like most other women by all accounts, that 90% of the male population are complete tossers, while the other 10% are just sufferable. I found myself having to agree with Nuala's assessment of the male population, especially when I considered how closely it mirrors men's opinion of women.

So boys and girls! If you decide to make a commitment, it might be a good idea to base your decision on respect, and not as so often is the case on something as unreliable as romantic love. Also acknowledge each others differences and try not to become too complacent, while wrapped in the security of such a commitment.

Acknowledgements

I wish to thank the following people who unbeknown to themselves have contributed so much to this book.. Madge & Billy, Christine & Adam, Liz G, Patrick & Fran, Fr V Kennedy, J Hannigan, S Cullen, D Cronin, D Scurry, Annette S, The McKenna family, Bernie Q, Emer L, Rachel T, Sinead K, Stephen & Joni, R Stafford, Debbie C, Martin & Mary, Willie & Catharine, Sandra & Tommy, G Buckley, John & Mairéad, Loraine & Nuala, K Hobson, D Cassidy.

"References"

John Grays *(2002) Men are from mars, women are from Venus*

Gary Goldschneider, Joost Elffers (2004) The secret languages of birthdays

Allan Pease (2002) Why men lie and women cry

Suzanne White (1987) The new astrology

Stephan Arnott & Mike Haskins (2004) Man walks into bar

Help lines & Web sites

Alcoholics Anonymous:... 01-4538998

Al-anon. Al-anteen:... 01-8732699

AMEN: help for male victims of domestic abuse.... 046-9023718

Aware: depression support.............................. 1890-303302

Bereavement counselling services:..................... 01-8391766

Irish cancer society... 1800-200700

Child Line.. 1800-666666

Cot Deaths I.S.I.D.A..................................... 1850-391391

Cura: Support through crisis pregnancy................ 01-6710598

Cherish: Single parent family support................. 01-6629212

Drugs/H.I.V Helpline:.................................... 1800-459459

Gamblers Anonymous:.................................... 01-8721133

Gay Switch Board:... 01-8721055

Gingerbread: association of one parent families...... 01-8146618

M.O.V.E: Men Overcoming Violent Emotions........ 01-8724357

Parent Line: Parents under Stress...................... 1890-927277

Rape Crises Centre:.. 1800-778888

Samaritans:.. 1850-609090

Sexual Abuse Services..................................... 01-8335044

Separated persons association of Ireland...............01-8720684

Victim Support.. 1850-661771

Unmarried & separated fathers of Ireland.............01-4516227

Samaritans:....................................www.samaritians.org

Suicide bereavement:.......................mailto:nsbsn@eircom.net

Aware: sufferers of depression............http://www.ias.ie

Gingerbread...................................www.gingerbread.ie

AMEN...www.amen.ie

It's time for me to take my leave, but before I go I'd like to take this opportunity to enhance the chances of all you singletons out there, to meet that "special" person. So over the next two pages I've included a few well known ice-breakers accompanied by some of the responses you are likely to receive from the "ice-berg" if you happen to overstay your imaginary welcome.

**AND
IF THESE DON'T WORK LADS
YOU'RE ON YOUR OWN !**

"ICE BREAKERS"

Tell me about yourself-your struggles, your dreams and your phone number.

Can you do C.P.R? You're taking my breath away.

That dress looks nice, would you mind if I tried talking you out of it?

What's a nice girl like you, doing in my dirty mind?

That dress would look great crumpled up on my bedroom floor.

Is that seat empty? "Yes, and so will mine if you try sitting on it".

Do you want to go back to my place? "Will the two of us fit under your rock?"

What's your sign? "Keep moving"

Is there any chance we can go to my place, to do the things I'm going to tell people we did anyway?

I'd do anything for you, "try disappearing".

Have we met before? "Possibly, I work at the local S.T.D clinic"

What do you work at? "I'm a bull-shit tester"

I'm very sorry, I thought that was a Braille name tag.

Are you from outer space? "Why" because your ass looks out of this world.

Do you believe in love at first sight, or should I walk past again?

Excuse me, I've just noticed you noticing me, so I'm just letting you know, that I noticed you too.

I've been undressing you with my eyes all night long, "no wonder I'm feck'n freezing".

What's your number? "It's in the phone book" but I don't know your name? "That's also in the phone book".

A man flying to New York is seated next to an absolutely gorgeous woman. He notices the woman is reading a book containing various sexual statistics and he decides to ask her about it. "It's a very interesting" she says. "It seems American Indians have the longest penises, while Irish men have the widest. By the way, my name is Helga. What's yours? The man replies 'Tonto Maguire"

"And some icy responses"